MICROCOSM·PUBLISHING

MICROCOSM PUBLISHING is Portland's most diversified publishing house and distributor, with a focus on the colorful, authentic, and empowering. Our books and zines have put your power in your hands since 1996, equipping readers to make positive changes in their lives and in the world around them. Microcosm emphasizes skill-building, showing hidden histories, and fostering creativity through challenging conventional publishing wisdom with books and bookettes about DIY skills, food, bicycling, gender, self-care, and social justice. What was once a distro and record label started by Joe Biel in a drafty bedroom was determined to be *Publishers Weekly*'s fastest-growing publisher of 2022 and #3 in 2023 and 2024, and is now among the oldest independent publishing houses in Portland, OR, and Cleveland, OH. We are a politically moderate, centrist publisher in a world that has inched to the right for the past 80 years.

The following was composed by people who organize squatted dance parties in the U.S. today. The link between unauthorized dancing and radical politics extends back many decades, from the early rave scene and the worldwide squatting movement through Reclaim the Streets and Occupy. Even if you live in a small Midwestern town far from the dances of New York City and the squats of Athens, Greece, you can still organize adventurous escapades that demonstrate how much more joyous life could be. The ways we contest the ruling order should always include an element of delight.

This guide was created before the COVID-19 pandemic began, so take the appropriate safety precautions—for example, you could hold your event in an open parking garage or in a clearing in the woods.

The fun in throwing an illegal party is above all in breaking out of the space and time of authority. For millennia, people of countless societies and walks of life have gathered to dance as a way of escaping the pressures placed on them. There is good reason for this! When intimacy is constrained or channeled into models of utility such as commerce, work, family, and the couple, dance parties offer the possibility of an intimacy that exceeds these constraints. Dancing also enables us to experience ourselves differently, to experiment with our bodies and open ourselves to joyous abandon beyond our prescribed social functions.

The flipside to this history is nearly as long. Club owners, social climbers, and bros capitalize on our desires or prevent us from being in touch with them. That's the reason to hold squatted dance parties: to open up a space beyond control.

> "The second floor was just one big open room. We brought a pile of old roller skates so people could roll around it. At two am, when the flames from the bonfire outside were almost licking the third floor balconies, we began throwing televisions off the roof."

LOCATION, LOCATION, LOCATION

First things first, you need a place for your party. You don't want to throw it at your house and all the conventional venues are boring and expensive. There are a few ways to solve this problem. In most major metropolises, you can find many buildings in tenuous conditions of ownership or management. Some buildings are straight up abandoned—they are owned by banks somewhere far away or by a landlord who inherited them decades ago and has never been to visit them. If you're planning to organize a squatted dance party, this is the kind of building you need to find.

Failing this, you could try to find an owner who will turn a blind eye for a night or rent you a place cheap. You don't necessarily need to be clear about what your plans are if the owners don't pay attention to the space.

If you decide to squat, you need to take the location of the building into account. Look for a place that's concealed from public view but still located centrally enough that people will come to it. You don't want random cars or pedestrians passing by who might report your event to the police. Deindustrialization has left a ton of buildings like this in its wake; you shouldn't have too much trouble finding something. If you need help finding a place, reach out to local graffiti kids—they probably have some leads.

If you plan to keep the address secret until the day of the party, you have a bit of time to procrastinate when it comes to finding a space. But don't wait too long to figure it out—the party has to happen somewhere.

> "Crossing the river on the sketchy old catwalk, we reached a vast metal and concrete structure that had once been used to load barges. The previous generation of punks had held generator shows there. It was perfect for our plan."

GEARING UP

Once you've got a space, you need to fill it up with sound.

You can determine how much sound equipment you need according to the size of the space. If it's the size of a living room, a couple of 12" speakers will do. If it's any bigger, you want to start thinking about adding bass speakers to beef up the low end. You should also consider the shape of the space so that you can ensure that there is sound everywhere. Maybe you want to put a speaker or two in the back of the room to fill it out a bit more.

Unfortunately, sound equipment is not easy to come by. In most cases you'll need to own it, rent it, or borrow it from a friend. Hopefully, you've made connections in whatever scenes you have access to. Borrow the PA used at all the punk shows and those CDJs used at the hip hop gigs.

The prerequisite for music, lighting, fog, and practically everything else you need is—electricity. Arranging this can be a bit tricky. If your event is at an abandoned warehouse in the woods with no power source nearby, you'll need a generator. You can rent one at Lowe's or Home Depot. Make sure to test it beforehand to make sure it can do what you need it to—you don't want the power to cut out when you're deep in the mix! As long as you don't run the cords too far and you aren't counting on it to power 6 subwoofers and some laser light shit, you should be fine. When you're using a generator, you want to aim for minimalism: accomplish as much as you can with as little gear as possible.

Alternatively, you could borrow electricity from somewhere on the grid nearby. Maybe you know the folks who work at the business next door and they're willing to let you run extension cords over to the spot. Maybe you don't know the neighbors but there's an open outlet. Just make sure they're not going to pull the plug midway through your event! Sometimes you can find working outlets around public utilities. In Brazil, the organizers of guerrilla punk shows used to scale light posts to tap into the electrical grid to power PA systems—but if you are not a professionally trained electrician, don't risk your life trying a stunt like this.

> "Sometimes we would rent out the skating rink. The owners didn't care what went on there. People would bring bikes, skateboards, shopping carts, and a sound system."

DRAWING A CROWD

Now you're ready for the final ingredient, which is also the most important one: people!

The high point in any moment of social upheaval coincides with a general indiscernability of the participants involved. The same is true of a good party.

You want to create a situation in which different sorts of people feel that the conditions are present for them to do whatever they want. This doesn't mean denying differences; it doesn't mean appealing to the lowest common denominator or establishing some sort of middle ground compromise—no one actually likes tech-house. Rather, it means creating ways for people to engage on their own terms, to participate in the practices that they most enjoy, with the people they actually want to be with.

When you're promoting your event, think outside your immediate social milieu. If you don't have access to a particular scene, organize with people who do. You could make multiple flyers with different aesthetics, or book DJs that play different styles of music. That said, don't muddy up the event too much aesthetically; above all, you want to send a simple yet profound message about what the night will hold. Your invitation should intrigue people, casting a spell that makes them expect a lot of it and of themselves. The goal is to make sure that your event spills over the threshold of normalcy. The distinction between a decent party and a great one is not just a matter of how skilled the DJ is—it is a question of how far the participants are willing to go to forget about society and all the rules it imposes.

> "We would drive around the suburbs collecting discarded Christmas trees off the curbs until we had a massive stockpile. Then we would build huge wooden structures to set on fire. One year, my friends erected a 'Tower Against God and Science' and everyone wrote messages on it before we set it ablaze."

PROMOTION

Assuming your party is illegal to some degree, you should take precautions in promoting it so that you don't catch a case after the fact. If you are promoting your event through social media, do so anonymously. Make a Facebook profile using Tor browser, and verify the account with a burner phone paid for in cash. Create a new name for your party or party promoting entity so that it's harder to single out any particular individual as the one responsible for organizing the event. After you've created the event, ask people to share it so you can make use of the social media networks you already have access to.

Print out flyers for your event and wheatpaste them where the people you want to draw will see them. Visit all the collective houses you know about and spread the word.

It may make sense to conceal the address of your party or other such details until the day it occurs. On the day of the event, you could use an anonymous twitter account to broadcast the location, or set up an anonymous email address to auto-respond to inquiries with those details, or arrange for people to spread the word through Signal messages and rumors. If this is your plan, make sure you've spread the twitter or email account from the very beginning.

> "Many Roman squats came out of raves, momentary dance parties held in unusual places. In the 1990s they did raves in gardens and abandoned buildings. This started in 1994, and was mobilized by radio. "If you happen to be in this district tonight…" They went into one factory and danced for hours on a carpet of discarded photocopy toner. They only knew

it when the sun rose and they saw each others' blue faces."

-"Squatters of Rome"

BE PREPARED

*E*ven if you're just squatting the place for the duration of the dance, bring a first aid kit and a fire extinguisher and mark the fire exits if applicable. Invite your street medic friends; ideally, someone should have first responder training. If you're creating a situation in which anything can happen, and you want it to be a good experience for the participants, make sure you really are prepared for anything to happen. This is part of being capable of maintaining truly autonomous spaces.

Lastly, and unfortunately, you should consider how to handle the authorities. Prepare a plan for dealing with the police if they come to your event. Go over this together with all the other organizers so everyone agrees on how to respond and feels prepared.

Rule number one: if the police show up, don't let them in. They'll pretend that they have a right to enter; they might say they "just want to check it out." Don't fall for it! Don't let them in. Give them an inch and they'll take a mile. If you have to, play for time—you could give them the number for a voice mail or a burner phone with a friend on the other end of it representing the owner of the space. Generally speaking, you want to volunteer as little as possible, to avoid things getting more complicated.

Consider having your vegan straightedge friends work the door so if the cops show up, there are sober, assertive people prepared to keep them out. They still might manage to get inside somehow, so prepare an emergency plan in advance to deal with that scenario. If there is an impromptu bar or something like that functioning inside, make sure people are ready to disassemble it and rush everything out a back door at a given signal. If there are people in more vulnerable legal situations—undocumented, on probation, etc.—make sure that they are able to exit safely, too. You should also have a plan to get the speakers and other expensive gear out of there!

IF THE POLICE SHOW UP

If the police address you, ignore them unless they specify that you are being detained or arrested. If they seize you, don't resist unless you're sure you can escape; resisting can get you higher charges. If you are arrested, invoke your right to remain silent. Answer no questions beyond your name and address, no matter what they say. Never tell the police anything about other people, even if it seems insignificant.

Don't post anything on social media or any other site that you wouldn't show directly to the police. Don't brag about anything potentially incriminating, or describe others' actions. Only talk about what happened in a secure environment with people you trust.

The corporate media will repeat the lies of the police. Politicians will try to discredit you or get you to waste time in endless petitioning. Don't let them intimidate you or stunt your imagination; don't get sucked into a private grudge match with the authorities. Power comes from our courage, our dreams, and the connections we build with other people.

SUBSCRIBE!

For as little as $15/month, you can support a small, independent publisher and get every book that we publish—delivered to your doorstep!

www.Microcosm.pub/BFF